FINANCIAL INTELLIGENCE

ACHIEVING FINANCIAL INDEPENDENCE
INVESTING AND BUILDING WEALTH IN OUR CULTURE
FINANCIAL SYSTEMS FOR FINANCIAL FREEDOM

KWABENA OBENG DARKO

E-mail your questions and comments to the author at:

info@obengdarko.com.gh

www.obengdarko.com.gh

Designed and Printed and Published by:

Odtrah

P . O . BOX MS 13

Mile 7-Achimota

Accra-Ghana

TEL: +233 24 6631874

FINANCIAL INTELLIGENCE

ACHIEVING FINANCIAL INDEPENDENCE
INVESTING AND BUILDING WEALTH IN OUR CULTURE
FINANCIAL SYSTEMS FOR FINANCIAL FREEDOM

KWABENA OBENG DARKO

DEDICATION

This book is dedicated to Africans who want financial freedom.

AUTHOR'S NOTES AND ACKNOWLEDGMENT

My wife, Marie and children, Yaa, Awuraa and Kwabena.
My parents and siblings

CONTENTS

Dedication
Acknowledgement
Introduction

INTRODUCTION

Financial success requires financial systems and to be able to build financial systems you need some level of financial intelligence. Systems are principles that make things happen. Systems are processes that work together to bring certain results. You must have your financial systems that work to bring you financial freedom over a certain period. It takes financial intelligence to get this done. The world runs on systems and wealth creation takes systems. Problems are solved with systems and so are financial problems with financial systems. It takes financial intelligence to understand financial systems and those who understand financial systems easily achieve financial freedom. Culture is an educational system. It becomes very challenging to see wealth in your culture without a proper understanding of your culture. If your sense of history is wrong your understanding of yourself will be wrong. Once your sense of history is wrong your education becomes limiting. The depth of your history and your understanding of your culture. Pay attention.

Many of us may not have easily identifiable gifts or talents that bring notoriety and financial success, like musicians, footballers, actors, etc. Those of us without these obvious talents must focus on developing our crafts and minds. Many of us are artisans and many of us may have intellectual abilities, especially those with higher education. Both must develop our abilities as we improve our financial intelligence. Building financial independence requires financial intelligence development. It takes time to build such intelligence and without building it we miss the opportunity to have financial freedom. A state where money does not restrict our choices.

It is very tough to have financial freedom without financial intelligence. The ability to solve problems has a lot to do with our intelligence and being able to solve our financial problems has much to do with our financial intelligence. Many problems are humanly created and it takes humans to solve many of the problems that we meet in life and financial problems are not excluded. Those who succeed financially don't just hope and wish their finances will change one day.

- They acquire the right financial education

- Develop the right financial mindset

- Build the right financial skill set

- They structure their finances

- They work to have financial freedom

Financial freedom brings you options in life. You can control your time and aspirations if you have financial freedom.

- Plan for financial freedom

- Give yourself at least 10 years

- It takes financial discipline

- It takes financial skills

- It takes courage

School as we have it has trained our people to become job seekers and so when they complete school they wait for the government or others to employ them. Train people to be proud of who they are and their heritage, they will not wait for others to come and help them. They will help themselves and they will cherish freedom and dignity. Once we start to organize the minds of our people they will start to take charge of our resources. Processing and manufacturing using our numerous natural resources will become our priority. Some level of financial intelligence is needed for people to take hold of their resources.

Don't be overly careful and don't be afraid of taking risks to gain your financial freedom.

- Goals

- Culture

- Resilience

- Persistence
- Cash flow
- Budget
- Assets
- Liability
- Investment

Build the base so that your financial future can be right. Most people, especially the educated, know how to read and write, they are technical. They have professions, they are engineers, they are accountants, and nurses. They are literate, but very few people have financial literacy. They may be professionals, have skills, and know a lot, but very few have educated themselves financially. Yet, they all believe that once they work and get money, they should be financially successful. It does not seem to work that way. Our choices and our decisions come from the things that we've been constructive about, the things that we have learned intentionally. So if you have not studied money intentionally, if you are not literate in terms of finance, your choices and decisions will eventually sell you out.

You will see that you will struggle financially, your financial plans, your financial decisions and your choices will not be right. When you work to get money or when you even do business and you get the money, the decisions that you make on money will be direct products of the financial education, the financial literacy that you have acquired yourself.

Everybody has a fair chance to be financially free if we have the right financial education and the right financial information. So financial intelligence is very much crucial for our financial success.

Ultimately, intelligent financial decisions are responsible for financial success. Financial success does not just happen. It is intentional and it must be well planned and executed. There must be long-term planning, discipline and consistency. Personal financial skills development, hard work, great work ethics, sacrifices and patience should not be left out.

.

CHAPTER 1

ॐ

FINANCIAL INTELLIGENCE

Intelligence requires that we understand the environment we live in and how it operates. There should not be a separation between what you know and what works financially in your environment. Financial intelligence requires that we understand our financial environment, how it works, and what it takes to be financially successful in it.

The more you improve your financial intelligence the more you see the danger in depending on one source of income which is not enough to take care of you. You start to see the options available that can easily help you to have multiple sources of income. Many opportunities fall within trading and agriculture. The problem is not that many are poor. The problem is that many lack financial intelligence. Many cannot organize their finances. It is not how small you start your journey to financial freedom, it is about having a financial plan and sticking with it till it starts to make sense. One of the challenges we have as a people is that many of us don't study the financial systems we have. Many who even read financial books read those from different economic structures and so the application of the things they learn from those books becomes difficult. What they see on the ground is different from what they learn in school or what they read in the books. It is your responsibility to acquire the right financial education that applies in our environment and that is what will bring you financial independence. For most of us, our struggles come from how we handle our finances. If our finances are struggling, almost every aspect of the business will continue to struggle. We handle the business money as we understand money. So if you don't know better, you will not be able to do better. The moment we get the right information, we probably start to make the right decisions with the finances of the business.

Most of us, our struggles come from how we handle the finances. If our finances are struggling, almost every aspect of the business will continue to struggle.

When you owe and you refuse to pay the people and run away you have a problem with money. Treating debt as something that you have to run away from, you have financial challenges. So if you're like that, then you're going to struggle with money, because your character is a problem. Money problems usually is a character problems. So if your character is right, if you have the right information, maybe you may not be a billionaire, maybe you may not be a millionaire, but you'll be able to have your finances right through pushing yourself in the best of practices.

Education is built on what the people know and understand, the culture of the people. The world runs on money and you must be aware of that. You should also know that it is your responsibility to be financially free. Don't wait for help and don't wait for anybody to make you financially free.

- Your financial intelligence is seen in how you solve financial problems and so those with strong financial intelligence are people who are well skilled in solving problems.

- They are determined to succeed financially as well and they are skilled in communicating and dealing with people.

- They embrace risk, manage losses well and have strong emotional stability.

- Develop the right mindset for financial success.

- Build the right skill set for financial success.

Financial freedom helps to have no or little restrictions when it comes to your finances with the lifestyle you have.

CHAPTER 2

∾

SUCCESS HABITS

―――――――――

Your habits have contributed largely to wherever your life is at the moment. Your money habits have decided whether you are rich or poor. What you know has formed our habits and our habits about money have determined the decisions that we make with the money that has come to us.

Many people who work for a salary think if they have their salary increased their finances will get better, which could be true. But what makes the difference is not the increase but how they handle money. Some get salary increases but they also increase their expenses, thinking that for people to know they have money they must look better or rich. Those who have money have different habits when it comes to money that is why they have money and those who don't, have different habits with money, many times poor money habits. For food, clothing and shelter you should be able to afford them and have excess money at the level of the lifestyle you have carved for yourself. Financial success comes in different levels. You can be comfortable, rich or wealthy. Each calls for a different financial lifestyle, capacity and freedom.

What is important is you are happy and fulfilled with the life you have and the money needed to keep the life.

Based on your lifestyle you can achieve financial freedom at each level.

Financial freedom is where you don't have to work for money to have food, clothing and shelter. Where you don't have to work for money to live. Where you don't have to work for money to have security and health. Financial freedom is where money works for you and you can be happy with the level of financial lifestyle you have. Keep your discipline and your level until you have an allowance for the next level.

Financial Success Habits

1. If you continue to owe and cannot pay back you have poor financial habits.

2. Those with great financial success habits don't wish that their debt will be magically cancelled.

3. They structure their finances and have control over their finances.

4. They continually educate themselves about finances and they don't have to borrow to eat.

5. They tell themselves the truth about their finances. They

have a full understanding of their financial situation.

6. They have financial goals. They track their money and they have a budget.

7. They don't just hope that they will prosper.

8. They work to see success.

9. People who continually succeed financially have financial success habits.

10. They go for proper financial education all the time. When others who struggle with money are obsessed with entertainment, they commit to personal development and financial literacy. This is one of the main reasons they are successful with their finances. They are not superstitious about money.

11. They believe if they plan their finances well they will succeed. And they do succeed.

12. They know when the money is coming in, where it is going and what it is going to do.

13. Those with financial success habits pay those they owe. They don't forget their debt. They have a strong value system with money.

14. They build different sources of income such that what they receive is far more than what they need for their

lifestyle.

15. They save money, multiply money and constantly look for ways to invest their money.

16. Their close relationships have strong money habits as well. They don't play games with money.

17. They take full responsibility for their finances.

18. They don't leave their financial life or future to chances or luck. They are intentional about their finances.

19. They have proper financial goals and they do everything possible to reach them, both short-term financial goals and long-term financial goals. They are not wasteful with money. And they budget their money.

When others are afraid to take financial risks those with success habits take risks and are very good managers of their time. They don't play or waste their time. They fully understand the value of time. One remarkable thing about them is that they are very tough, consistent and resilient people. They are not the kind that you can easily push over when it comes to achieving their financial goals. No matter how many times they fall they get back up to fight again and they are very much flexible with their approach in getting to their financial goals. That is why they are successful.

CHAPTER 3

TEACHINGS

If you want many of our people to like you don't talk about religion. People can like us and be that friendly until they get to see you don't have the same thinking or view on how religion is practised in our country. You easily become an enemy of God and yet religion is part of the things that have put many of our people to sleep or in bondage. They want to solve financial problems with prayer.

1. Financial success takes more than prayer.
2. It takes work.
3. It takes the decisions you make with money.
4. How you invest money.

The teachings and the practices make our people not see how they are responsible for what happens in their lives or how our country develops. This has been one of the reasons many people hardly develop the right financial mindset and skill set. They have been taught that there is another realm in the spirit where we have no control as we are mainly made to believe. The teachings on the afterlife make us not commit to doing something significant while we are alive because the world is coming to an end or we are going to die and go to a better place. People become what they are taught or what is pressed on their minds dominantly or consistently. We seem to forget that even if we die now, we leave others behind who need money to go through life.

Many times I ask myself, why do we expect our people to develop or build our country where religion has dominated almost every discourse. We seem not to hold people to higher standards, we only have to satisfy ourselves that this person has the same faith as us. Religion can easily be weaponised to put people into poverty and bondage and we can see many churches and mosques across the length and breadth of our country. What frees the people is truth and love for one another.

Anybody can start a church and begin to teach our people anything so long as they say that God called them. We need to do a lot of work to get to see many of our people to see religion as an entity that gives hope and develops character and not a way to renege our duties to the divine while we just do what we want

The quality of knowledge available to a people decide how they see themselves and how they see the world and interact with it.

hoping our finances will be taken care of by God. That is why people are made to believe that they will be rich even though they have no or little financial knowledge or skills. Just because nothing is impossible with God as they are told all the time. Our country will be developed as we pray and fast as if God will be the one to build our schools, clean our gutters, educate our people, build roads and start businesses or farms. It is not the responsibility of humans to create the Earth or the Universe and it is not the duty of God to build cars or computers. Cars and computers are built by humans with the right knowledge and expertise. The quality of knowledge available to people decides how they see themselves and how they see the world and interact with it.

In the time we live in with the advancement of science and technology, we cannot interpret critical development factors with religion as it is clear that countries that are committed to innovation, science, engineering, technology and entrepreneurship are the ones building factories and industries. We have got to look at religion again in our country, especially Christianity and Islam and the critical mental development of our people. For our development we should not be afraid for anyone to question these religions and their impacts on our ability to innovate, think, structure and build our country.

It is almost impossible to have the African think rightly about Africa until the religion is practised rightly with love, truth and compassion. Even those doing a little better, just motivate us but the required skills, the environment and the resources needed to bring development and not given the needed attention. Motivation is different from having the right capacity to get results. Most often, it is the capacity of the minds, hearts, hands and legs that we have not built. Do we know how to get the results? Seeing the advantages that you have requires that you get your religion right, not manipulated, fear-driven and hoping for a better tomorrow without any strategy skills or resources. Proper development of financial intelligence can be devoid of the issues of faith and fate.

CHAPTER 4

AFRICAN MIND

Many of our people think that colonization happened a long time ago and it has no effect on how we live our lives today as Africans. I have heard many people say that it happened, it stopped and Africans cannot continue to blame others and we should move on. If you look at the countries in Africa do you really believe that they live freely and are developing their people and their various countries by their own structures?

In Ghana what we call formal is largely based on British or European culture. Even writing in English as an Asante man shows the distortions that we are dealing as a people. The development of our language, culture, religion, politics, etc have been largely affected by our interaction with the Europeans and they did not seek for our development as such.

The dangerous aspect is even the way we think of ourselves as a people when we meet other race especially those who practiced colonization. Many Africans has been trained to look up those as a god or as savior through school and religion mainly. We look up to God or the colonisers to save us. It is in our conditioning. We have been brainwashed not to lift ours or develop ourselves but to look to them to save us. You have to make deliberate decision to decolonize your mind as an African so that you can see yourself as able and that your people are trustworthy, intelligent and are capable of solving their own problems to develop. It takes a lot of effort to do this because many of our own people will even fight you if you start to speak well of Africans or if you start to believe in Africa and Africans.

Developing strong African sense will require we build Africans who see themselves as Africans. Africans who are proud of their language, their names, their culture, their future and are very positive about Africa.

The minds of many of our people need to be worked on to accept themselves and be proud of themselves. The way we see ourselves as Africans is one of our major problems because the average African does not have a high sense of self value especially when they compare themselves with those who came to the Continent to pillage us through their indoctrination. Many of our people would love to move out of Africa and many believe they will have a far better life if they go to these so-called developed countries. Our confidence in our ability to work to develop our continent is something we have to build in the youth of Africa.

Many look up to political leadership and blame them for everything that is not right. There is more to the things we deal with and much of it is structural. How our various countries have been set up, our political systems that don't fit the cultures that we have, financial systems that don't work for the prosperity of our people and even the way we are educated.

Once you are able to rework on your mind as an African you start to feel proud of yourself and your heritage and your people. You will become patient with us and you will start to make an effort for us to do well and prosper. You start to want to see your people in charge of innovation and industries in your countries

Decolonization of the African mind is a lifelong journey because the very institutions that perpetuate this are still alive and working on the minds of our people. This is at the foundation of your development as an African. Many of our people live in frustration and negativity

You don't need to teach the African about financial intelligence if the mind of the African has not been restored. Until the African is proud of himself or herself.

because they have not decolonized their minds as Africans. Build the African in you and you will be a proud productive African. Read history beyond slavery and colonization, that is what worked for me. Great African history is what you need to decolonize your mind as an African. You don't need to teach the Africans about financial intelligence if the minds of the Africans have not been restored. Until the African is proud of himself or herself.

CHAPTER 5

FINANCIAL SYSTEMS

Financial success is systemic and our understanding of the financial systems that we operate in has a lot to do with our financial achievements. Your ability to improvise your financial system within the financial structures that you operate in will go a long way on your journey to financial freedom. People often compare our financial structure with other countries. What you must know is our financial systems are very different. Others may operate with debt for almost everything, from personal finances to business finances to even investments. We may not have these debt structures but we may have something that works if you will take time to understand what we have.

One thing that we usually see is how those with different financial infrastructures always bulk all of us into financial and wealth classifications when we don't have the same systems and supports. There are different technological differences and different institutions and regulations. You will reduce a lot of errors and frustrations when you start to analyze these different economic structures in Africa and that of the so-called developed economies. We should build our models and classify our wealth based on what is available to us. Africans are not poor it is the tools that they are using to judge Africans and Africa. Don't buy these lies. Educate yourself. Study these different financial systems and work with what we have you can easily be wealthy in Africa if you know the differences. How you even structure your business and investments will change once you can understand the

> *Don't let the system keep you from having your financial freedom*

differences in the financial systems. One is debt and the other is mainly cash and goodwill. Don't let the system keep you from having your financial freedom and you can do that if you gain the required financial intelligence. Many structures have been designed to keep people poor and average and those systems will continue to keep them in bondage until they gain the understanding of these systems through financial education. The financial education needed to free you is not complicated. Eschew a lot of these complicated and technical financial instruments. They are designed to keep many from gaining financial freedom. While you have strength focus on investing thing businesses and entities that will give you money when you can no more work with your strength. Don't forget your retirement age. That age will come.

One of the ways that many don't gain financial freedom is the confidence in degrees and certificates and dependence on jobs and salaries. That is a system. Use your intellectual skills from your degrees to educate yourself financially and use your salary as seen to build your financial freedom. Real financial freedom comes from businesses and investments.

Study these different financial systems as you build your wealth, businesses or investments. Many Africans don't study the differences and so they insistently compare and put themselves down in their quest to seek livelihood and financial freedom. Many of the instruments that they have built them great business growth and investments are not readily accessible or are non-existent to many of our people, from venture capital money, equity funding, stock market, funds from real estate investment, start-up supports, numerous financial applications and technologies, numerous money market and capital market categories.

We should focus on the level of financial technologies available to us. Also, the businesses we can easily do and become successful, bearing in mind the demands in our market and building with what we have. Extend your tentacles but never overlook the numerous opportunities that are available to us in the financial systems that we have. Once you understand this your approach to building businesses and investments in our system will improve and start to see significant results.

- International payment business systems have excluded a large part of African business.

- Financial laws that only promote their interest

- Money for budding businesses

- Money for business growth

- Shares, Stocks, IPOs

- Control of mineral prices

- Etc.

How many of us are using IPOs or the Stock Market to expand our businesses? A lot of these things don't apply to so many of our people in business, the reason you must focus on what is available to you at your level and business from there.

CHAPTER 6

FINANCIAL EDUCATION

There was a time we visited one of our project sites and saw this man and his wife there, they had built their own house. We happened to know them somewhere. They had a provision shop, and out of the provision shop, they had been able to build a house and also built and opened shops in front of their new house as well. They are not people that you would say are so highly educated. No, but at least they have been able to do something for themselves. There is another young man we know. He makes about GH₵ 3000 a month from the work he does. He has been able to accumulate money and he wants to travel to another country and nothing that you tell him that he would agree to. While some others have been able to focus and build houses and open businesses others are looking at getting out of the country. It comes down to the mindset that people develop over time. r him, no matter how well he's doing, he still wants to move to America before he feels like he is worthy. So you can see a doctor doing well, but he will still want to move and become a nurse somewhere. He thinks that these pounds and dollars will make them successful. That's not true. The difference is in the financial plans that we have. That's not how you build wealth. You can buy a house and buy a car over all these years that you trade your hours for it with a lot of disrespect and unfair treatment as an African in a lot of these countries. This means a lot of us don't understand how to have a financial plan for our future. You must develop a plan that will take about 3 to 10 to 20 years and work with it. Having a plan for your finances is so critical, it's so important. Growing up, most of us would think that if we traveled to other countries, it would mean that we would have escaped poverty. Without you having your financial plan, without you having your financial structure to get out of poverty, life will be tough. All of us need to have an understanding that for us to win financially, we must have financial education and financial plan.

Apart from those who have done some bit of finance in school, who are familiar with financial terms and financial principles and money loss, a lot of us have no clue about the principles of money. A lot of us don't know anything about money. We just work for salary, maybe we buy a car, house, clothes, and hope that the pension scheme will take care of us when we grow old. So financial literacy is very much key to your financial future and your prosperity. Those of us who are Christians, only pray for us to become rich, yet our education on money is weak. Our financial education is weak. Many are illiterate when it comes to money, and that's why most of us struggle all our lives with money. So financial education is that important. It allows you to make informed and quality decisions with money. Your understanding of what it takes to acquire money and how to grow the money is critical. Your financial education should help you to plan your finances.

Your plan must include your savings

- Your income sources

- Your savings

- Your cash flow

- Your investments

- Etc.

Your financial plan is critical and informs the decisions and the choices that you make with money. A lot of us don't even understand when we take loans, the implications of the interest on the loan, and the repayment structure that they give us. A lot of us don't know.

Those of us who do business should track the money that comes to us, bookkeeping, or knowing how the money is coming and how we are spending money. We don't even put down the expenses that we incur doing the business. They all come from the kind of education, the kind of understanding, the kind of information we have in terms of finances. We fail because we are not that deliberate.

We were not conscious with our finances. We have no plan. We just hope that things will improve. We will win sometimes then we will lose sometimes, because we have not been conscious, we have not been intentional with our financial education. We must have plan for our money.

So, I will employ you to study about the taxes in our country, study about cash-flow, how the money comes in. The business that you do, even if you work for salary. Don't wait to the end of the month to track how you spend that money.

- Do you know how much you spent on your transport?

- Do you know how much you spend going to that work?

- How much is your profit when they pay you?

- Do you make any money at all or you are in the negative?

When you're taking a loan, do you have any understanding of what the bank is charging? The bank charges and the insurance they put on them?

CHAPTER 7

MONEY MINDSET

Your mindset about money says a lot about how you handle money. What you do with money when it comes to you shows your money mindset. Do you so believe that you deserve to be wealthy? Those with a great money mindset don't give excuses. They are ready to do what they have to do to get ahead with their finances. They don't wait for someone to help them. They take full responsibility for their financial life. They are not hopeful that things will just change. They are not victims and don't look up to their government to solve their money problems for them. They continually educate themselves about money and they are disciplined with money. They don't wait for miracles. They take charge of their money situation. This is the kind of mindset you need to have financial success. They have goals and they expect results. A money mindset is focused on business opportunities. They focus on assets that generate income all the time. They don't waste their money and are not afraid of taking risks on their money that can lead to financial benefit. They look at long-term wealth.

Your money mindset should be a positive one. They are systemic in their money approach and they have plans for their money.

Your money mindset has to be right. No one thinking for them to have money some spirit must give them money. The right mindset solves money problems all the time. They manage their resources well and manage their time well. They are very resilient and do not relent in the quest to have their financial intelligence improve and ultimately have their financial freedom.

- Your money mindset should be that, no problem cannot be solved, even if not today. It only requires persistence and continual underdevelopment.

- Many people with the wrong money mindset are waiting for an economic savior. They are the ones always calling people to support them for their rent, children's school fees, etc.

- If you want to change your financial situation then build the right money mindset. You cannot win with the wrong money mindset. The reason many stay poor or struggle with money all their lives is because of the wrong money mindset.

- Those who win have the right mindset about money that is why they you. You think it is magic or lack and don't expect to have problems as you build your financial muscles. That is a wrong money mindset.

- Except problems. Expect challenges, but have goals, have strategies, and gain the needed financial information and you will ·see significant progress in your personal, family and business finances.

  As you practise. As you take financial risk. As you expose yourself the right financial information, your money mindset will grow and improve.

- Build the right financial and mental strength.

- You win or lose financially based on your money mindset.

- You don't develop this in the classroom. You develop this on the street. You develop this yourself. As you practice. As you take financial risk.

As you expose yourself to the right financial information, your money mindset will grow and improve. The rich man and the poor man don't have the same mindset on money. That is the fundamental difference between the rich and the poor. Their money mindset.

Knowledge is required for success and financial success demands deep knowledge. It is not about shallowness. The mind is a very powerful tool. You cannot win without developing this tool. You either build your life with it or you destroy your life with it. Your mind.

A weak mindset cannot win in life. A weak mindset hardly builds a strong spirit. Build a strong money mindset and you will be financially success.

It starts and ends with the mindset you have.

Money mindset, the difference between the rich and the poor.

CHAPTER 8

ରେ

FINANCIAL GOALS

O ur goals direct us and to become successful in anything we must have goals. Goals give birth to success. Our goals make us focused and driven. If you don't have financial goals then don't expect to have financial success. Many don't have any financial goals and that is why they have not seen much success with their finances.

- Have your own financial goals for the next year, the next two years, the next five years and the next ten years and so on.

- Have financial goals for your monthly income, profit and savings.

- Have goals for your yearly savings and investments.

- You cannot win until you set these goals and follow them.

- You can work on these goals as an individual and as a family.

- Once you start to hit your financial you start to see the world differently and start to have self-confidence and hope in your future.

- Not many who have their finances under control are frustrated and not useful in life

Where do you put your yearly savings and where do you put your yearly income? You can even do this monthly based on your level of income.

Where do you stand?

- GH¢0 to GH¢1000
- GH¢ 1000 to GH¢ 10,000
- GH¢ 10,000 to GH¢ 100,000
- GH¢ 100,000 to GH¢ 1,000,000
- GH¢ 1,000,000 to GH¢10,000,000
- Many more

Your financial freedom comes from the financial goals you have. If you have no goals you will struggle and it is as simple as such. If you don't have any financial goals then stop here, set your goals for the rest of the year before you continue.

Your financial goals will make you serious with your finances. Teach your children about the importance of having goals for your savings, income, investment and many more. Those who have financial goals are hardly wasteful with money. Hit your financial targets. Focus on your financial goals.

CHAPTER 9

~

MONEY SKILL SET

There are a set of skills that are needed to have money. The good thing is that these are skills that can be acquired once we are aware of them. Your ability to have income through your job or your business, being able to save money, knowing how to track the money that comes to you, the will to control how you spend money, being able to have a plan for your money and flowing it are all part to the skill set that you need to have money.

These skills are developed over time and those who have money have these skills. They may not be loud but they are practiced by many financially successful people. Having skills to set financial goals, having different sources of income, multiplying your income, being in the position to build investments that cash flow, investing in assets and not just spending money on things that don't bring money or increase in value over time.

Part of money skill set is entrepreneurship skills, being able to build a profitable business and the other skill is selling. Those who can sell products and services easily have money.

The other key skills are being hardworking and having great financial intelligence. The ability to make the right financial decisions is a skill and having emotional stability with money is part of the money skill set. Making the right investment decisions that end up positioning you to have passive income for a very long time is part of your money skill set. Not many people have these skills developed. You can see the results of the financial difficulties they go through almost all their lives. People skill is part of the money skill set. If you don't know how to walk with people who are successful in their field and those who make an effort to be successful it will be hard to do well financially. The blessing is in people. You are what you are largely because of the people you have known all your life. Your family, friends, workers, church members, party members, and so on. Don't take for granted your ability to connect with people. It is a great money skill. The ability to listen and learn from others is an important money skill. Financial success is a skill. Work on yours.

Lastly, the skill to keep upgrading yourself, adding value to yourself all the time. Becoming a person of value is a great money skill. If you develop yourself financially your finances will improve and never stop doing that.

CHAPTER 10

CREDIBILITY

Your character is your capital and those who build great finances build a great life of reputation. If you have to start life from a humble beginning then you must be a person who is truthful in your dealings. Have principles that you live with. Let people know that they can trust you can that must be more important to you than even money. Never sacrifice your credibility. You lose more in life and your finances when you are not credible. When your word can not be taken seriously you lose. There is so much you can get done if those you know or do business with know you as someone they can trust with their money or goods.

- There are so many who don't pay the people they owe but hoping to improve their finances. That is difficult. That is a step to financial freedom, not running away from those you owe.

- Don't be at the workplace changing documents that you have no business changing so that you can get money. You don't need to. If you are patient you can build with what you have.

- Walk with people who have credibility. People who have great ethics. Those who will not sacrifice their principle for financial gain.

The truth is that your credibility protects you from becoming poor or struggling financially. I have seen so many business people who have pulled all kinds of challenges because they have great life principles that they live by. Their yes is yes and their no is no. They are those who think they are smart by tricking people and being dishonest, they hardly do well continually. When other people start to see who they really are that is the point they begin to go down. Those who give them products stop to give them and those who give them money stop to do so. The reason is that they don't honor their promises. So people cannot count on them and so they stop introducing them to their networks. If you have to be in this situation, restart with credibility. Things will start to change. Pay those you owe. Correct the errors. Financial intelligence cannot be separated from your character.

- Keep your time.
- Keep your mind.
- Keep your word.

Your credibility is your ticket to your financial independence. Your financial greatness is your honesty.

CHAPTER 11

POSITIVE OUTLOOK

You need a positive attitude towards money if you are going to have any. Tough for a negative mind to have a positive life. There are so many problems and challenges in life that to have some peace you must make an effort to see the positive in many situations. If you are full of negativity you will give up on yourself and humanity. You can easily change your life by becoming a person who see the good side of life. You do not deny the problems and the challenges but you do not dwell on the negatives. It is very hard for the negative to be hopeful and keep trying. If you are not so much hopeful of striking gold why will you keep digging when you meet so many difficulties with no prospects of a good outcome?

A positive mind builds your life, skills and capacity. Those of you who are resilient in life are very much optimistic about life and that is why they succeed in life. Those who are positive in life have a certain high amount of self-

> *You can easily change your life by becoming a person who see the good side of life.*

esteem and self-acceptance. Negativity produces fearful tendencies in life but positive attitude produces high level mental energy that is required for success in anything including financial success. Learn to have positive thoughts.

The rich seem to have a lot of optimism about life. The poor many times are negative and fearful about life. You cannot keep trying if you are full of negativity. Financial success demands consistency, persistence, resilience, capacity, learnability and reliability and these things don't follow those who are overtaken with negativity.

- Positive minds produce a positive life

- Negative minds condemn before it even starts

- Positive minds express confidence

The world is negative towards Africa and many Africans have become negative towards Africa and their fellow Africans as well. The knowledge to be a positive African is not in school and it is not on TV. You must search for that knowledge that makes you become a positive African and a positive person towards Africa. It is tough to accept anything that has been continually described as bad, diseased and corrupt as positive. You must change these negative words about Africa and you will become a positive African. You will then start to see Africa in a positive light and that is the point you start to see the prosperity in Africa. From that moment you begin to experience and enjoy your blessing as an African.

NETWORKING

Connect with people who believe in you and who you are. When you have people around you who have your well-being at heart it affects how you see the world and how you see yourself and this affects your output in life. Your relationships have a direct impact on your results in life. One of the reasons people struggle in life is they don't have a good network of people who want them to succeed. Many people only have relationships with people who only come to see them because of what they get. When the very people around you only are interested in themselves you don't go far in life. You need people who are honestly adding value to you and creating opportunities for you to do well in life. People who are eager to share their contacts and resources with you so that you get ahead in your life, business, family, health and finances. You don't need people who are close to you to com-

> *You need people who are honestly adding value to you and creating opportunities for you to do well in life.*

pete with you and pull you down. In that case, it is better to be alone. You need people who share their knowledge and sources of their knowledge with you. People who don't hide what makes them better from you.

Your financial intelligence has a lot to do with your network, the people you connect. People who you know and people who know you. You have to intentionally develop such a network of people who have the kind of mindset about money and who are doing well financially or trying to do well financially. Success in life is about relationships. If you have created relationships you have a great life and if you have a bad relationship you meet a lot of difficulties in life and you struggle in life. The beauty and quality of life have a lot to do with the quality of your relationships and how intensely and selflessly they want you to be fulfilled and successful in life.

- Connect with positive minds

- Work with those who are developing themselves

- Connect with those with great ethics

- Network with positive minds

- Connect with proud Africans

Your network is your world and you can always build the world you want by working on your network.

CHAPTER 13

๛

CULTURE

<hr>

Your understanding of the culture you live in is as important as your understanding of yourself. Education without a proper understanding of your culture is very limiting. The intelligence of the people has a direct link to the culture of the people. Financial intelligence is being able to understand the financial culture. It is very tough to do business and succeed in a culture you do not understand. It is the people you are serving and how can you properly serve people you don't understand. The way the people think and do their things. Their aspirations, fears and beliefs must be studied and understood. Prosperity comes from productivity. Productivity is built out of a productive culture. The ability to get the work done comes from the training system that the people have been through. The culture is a training system and to get the best out of the people you must understand what have trained them. If the culture does not improve the lives of the people do not improve. The language that the people speak, what they eat, how they marry, how they work, etc.

One of the reasons many of the people who have been able to build businesses and a lot of investments in our country are not highly educated is that the more they get educated in our schools the more separated they become from the culture of the people. The more schooled they are the more they think the people should come up to a certain culture to qualify for their service. The people who don't have so many degrees are direct products from the level of the culture that the majority of the people are comfortable with and that is why they can come up with services and products that meet the people where they are. Success demands that you understand the people you are serving. It is not so much about so-called standards but about what the people know and are comfortable with and can afford it. If you can serve many people at a level that they are and at the price point they can afford you will succeed with your business. Unlearn the lies and learn the culture. It is hard to understand the flow of money in the culture if you don't understand the culture.

- So study the culture

- Be proud of your culture

- Master the culture

Your strength comes from the culture. You become weak if you are taken out of your culture. It is like taking the fish out of the water and expecting the fish to live. It can not.

Your nourishment, creativity and intelligence come from the very culture that developed you. You are at your best when you operate with this understanding.

If you want to find meaning in your life don't separate yourself from the culture that brought you up. If you want fulfillment in life, identify with your culture. The culture is an education structure. You want to be proud of yourself and your achievements then get to the culture. Study the financial intelligence of your grandparents and their parents. You will see that many of them had so much knowledge and wisdom. We just did not have the opportunity and learn their wisdom in our schools. No matter the destructions that others unleash on you if you are grounded in culture, your integrity will be in place. It is very easy less complicated and more impactful if you understand the culture and provide solutions that seem to fit the culture and lift the lives of the people.

• The culture is your uniqueness

• The culture is an education structure

• The culture is your backbone

• Your Financial culture is your financial intelligence. Study it well.

It is not only the success but how you overcome the failures and the debts.

CHAPTER 14

ᕫ

DIFFICULTIES

L earn to survive failure. Come out of financial difficulties to win. Many give up. Many blame the systems. Some blame their parents. Others blame their spouse. Their friends or their children. We all go through financial problems but those who can fight back, become successful.

It takes a lot of effort to build anything significant. One trait of strong financial intelligence is the ability to withstand very difficult financial challenges and be able to fight back to win. Your financial intelligence is tested in difficult times. When you meet serious financial problems do you give up or do you stay to fight back to win? That proves the level of your financial intelligence. It is not only the success but how you overcome the failures and the debts. The most difficult moments are when everything disintegrates.

There will be debt, there will be difficulties, and there will be problems. There would be challenges. Not all your workers are going to come back. There will be disintegration of the team. Sometimes even if you are a business partners and you go through some challenges your partner may not want to come back to the business again because not so many people are built for the stress, the pain, for struggles.

You cannot do much financially in life if you cannot deal with the numerous challenges on your financial independence journey. You will win if you don't give up because of financial problems be it debt or failure.

CHAPTER 15

ॐ

INCOME

———————————

The rich have difference sources of income. They don't depend on one source of income. A man with one is not far from taking Trotro now and then. The one source of income man is not far from being poor. The rich have multiple sources of income. Do you know how much you make every month?

- Is it less than GH¢ 1000 a month?
- Is it less than GH¢ 10,000 a month?
- It is less than GH¢ 100,000 a month?
- Is it less than GH¢ 1,000,000, etc?

Can you decide to increase the income you make within the next month? Do you know how much you make every year.

Can you multiply by say two? Can you make two times what you made last year this year? There is no limit on income. The only limit you have on your income is the limit you have placed on yourself. The beliefs you have about money. Your money mindset. Your money skill set. Those are the limiting factors. The financially intelligent are increasing their income all the time. They may have some falls but on the whole, they continuously increase their come.

They don't accept any limiting beliefs on their income at all. They are always innovating, they are always creating and they are always solving problems that fetch them money. They are in the game of income growth, while the poor and the average are protecting themselves from losing what they have. Tough to have money without having income sources and very difficult to depend on one source of income to have financial freedom.

Financial intelligence will make you not box your financial life and future on one source of income.

- Start a business
- Build skills that you can use to gain income
- Develop your selling skills
- You can look at agriculture
- You can look at trading
- You can look at what you can do on the internet
- Set at least GH¢ 1,000,000 income in a year target and work until you get there.
- If you have met GH¢ 1,000,000 income in a year then get to GH¢10,000,000, GH¢100,000,000, GH¢ 1,000,000,000, and so on.
- Build multiple sources of income.
- Keep growing. Keep pushing.
- Let us raise millionaires and billionaires in Ghana and Africa.

CHAPTER 16

SAVINGS

You make money by selling a product or service or by getting paid from your job. Your spending habits show how much you can save. There is a limit to how much you can save so always pay attention. You save money so that you can invest that which you save. If you want to be financially free you don't save the money for savings sake. Savings in this case is like the farmer keeping seed to sow. Keep money to invest for the money to multiply. We are not interested in saving money to pay rent, buy a car, and have a nice wedding or down payment for land you want to build a house on as a family house. We are talking about saving money as a technique to have money to invest.

You develop a plan for this savings. Look at how much percentage of your monthly income can be kept. Is it 10% of what comes to you every month or 20% or more? Whatever it is have a plan to keep the money that comes to you every day, every week, or every month. You will be impressed with how much you can save yearly if you so do this well. It is one of the best strategies to use to change your financial situation. If you cannot keep money then it will be hard to have money to invest. It does not matter how much you make, if you waste all, you cannot be financially stable.

- Make savings your habit.

- Make savings your lifestyle.

Look at your friends who always want you to waste your savings again.

Don't just save money. Save money to invest. That is the importance of savings.

The financially intelligent don't waste money.

- They preserve money.

- They keep money.

- Savings: keeping money to invest.

- Savings: not keeping money to spend.

- Protect the money that you save.

- Have control over what you save

- Have a structure that helps you to keep money

Those who don't have money have nothing saved. Those who struggle with money have bad habits with keeping money. Once money comes to them they destroy it. A farmer who cannot keep seeds has nothing to show.

BUDGETING

B udgeting has to do with your plan for the money that comes to you and how you spend that money. Just like any other thing, you don't need a lot of money before you start to have control over money or you start to have money. How you take care of the little money that comes to you shows whether you are going to have any or not. Budgeting is a tool to have control over your finances and it is a tool to financial independence. Money seem to have power over the minds of many people. They become intoxicated when they get money. Their minds refuse to function when they get money that they have never had before or money that they were not expecting. The reason you need a budget is it helps you to have some kind of control over the money that comes to you. Have a budget for your daily

Have a budget for your daily expenses, have a budget for your weekly expenses, have a budget for your monthly expenses and definitely have a budget for your yearly expenses.

expenses, have a budget for your weekly expenses, have a budget for your monthly expenses and definitely have a budget for your yearly expenses. If you know what you are going to use the money for before the money comes you will not waste or destroy it.

Budgeting helps with your money goals and it also helps you to control your money. It helps you from getting into unnecessary debt and spending money beyond your limit. It is very tough to have proper financial health if you don't know how to handle the money that comes to you. You are likely not to save money if you are weak in budgeting and you are unlikely to have any money to invest if you cannot manage the money that you receive from your job or business. Your financial confidence will start to go up once you structure your finances. It is a skill to have a budget for yourself and be disciplined enough to work with it. Those who don't have enough money are many times reckless with money. They have no financial regiment. They have no control over their money.

The reason the rich continue to have money is because they are not frivolous with money. They have structure for their money, what comes to them and what goes out. Money has a volatility tendency which is why you must have a structure to control it.

Have a budget for your money and you will do so much with what comes to you. There are so many people who don't have much income but have achieved so much in terms of how they have invested the money that comes to them. There are also so many who have so much money come to them who have no investment to show for all the money that has come to them over these while.

How to budget for all your significant money inflows and all your significant expenses, like buying a car, building a house, paying for education and so on. Budgeting is a financial freedom tool and it is a skill that you must master if you want financial freedom.

CHAPTER 18

ॡ

CASH FLOW

The reason many people suffer with their finances is because their cash flow is weak. The money that comes to them is far less than the money that goes out from them. Companies that do well have great positive cash flow and so they are able to pay their expenses and still have much left and that is why they do well. Those that do not do well have problems meeting their financial obligations. They can pay their salaries, their service providers, their rents, taxes and many others. The one who has financial freedom built with required financial intelligence is the person who sees money every day, every minute, every second more than what is needed

The moment you can generate more money than what you need you have strong cash flow and much of your financial problems will be over.

Focus on building strong cash flow.

- Which businesses can give you good cash flow

- Which investments can give you good cash flow

- Which jobs can give you good cash flow

It is not magic, those who have control over their finances have the intelligence to build strong cash flow. Good cash flow reduces your financial frustrations. In our economy, if you don't focus on cash flow you have no business. Very hard to depend on loans. They are too expensive and tough to have long-term investors as well. That is why project-based businesses that require so much capital injection before money starts to come from the business many times struggle while the young woman who sells at the market can build her business from that small beginning and succeed. You can pay those you owe when you have strong cash flow and you build trust because you can honour your promises. The reason many contractors go through a lot of financial difficulties is because of cash flow problems. They don't pay on time and they don't pay frequently. If you can see money every day you can easily solve your money problems.

Change your personal, family and business finances by focusing on building strong cash flow.

The rich are rich in cash they have strong cash flow.

Difficult to have financial freedom if you don't have a strong cash flow

Change your personal, family and business finances by focusing on building strong cash flow.

CHAPTER 19

MULTIPLICATION

Don't leave money idle. Find a way to grow the money that comes to you. If you don't multiply your money inflation you eventually eat that you keep that you don't find ways to grow. Find ways to make your money work for you. The way to multiply money is by making money work for you in tools like businesses and investments. The seed must be multiplied before it is eaten or you will not have any to plant or eat again. The same with money. If you eat what comes to you without multiplying it first you lose it and nobody becomes wealthy without multiplying the money that comes to them. They multiply them by doing business with the money or by investing the money in areas that multiply the money.

It takes a different kind of understanding to know and accept that money must be multiplied first before it is spent. If you make an excess of GH¢ 1000 every month, find a way to multiply that GH¢ 1000 before you use it to buy anything. Hold yourself for a while. Control the edge to always spend the money that comes to you first. If you have one business find a way to grow that business. Don't stay with one business or with a particular level of sales. Multiplication brings growth and whatever that we build we should see growth. Be happy with your progress no matter how little it may seem, but have a multiplication mindset.

- Multiply your knowledge level
- Multiply your sales
- Think in multiplication
- Strategize in multiplications.

Multiplication is abundance. There is no shortage of ideas or resources. There is no shortage of blessings. Be responsible in your abundance. Don't be wasteful in your abundance.

Financial intelligence requires that you think not in scarcity but in multiplication. The rich think in abundance.

Be responsible in your abundance. Don't be wasteful in your abundance.

There is always an opportunity to change your finances for the better. There is always an opportunity to be financially free. You just have to keep on becoming better and there is always an opportunity to become a better version of yourself.

Multiply your income. Multiply your businesses. Multiply your investments. Live in abundance.

CHAPTER 20

℘

LIABILITIES

―――――――――――――

Those who struggle with their finances spend a lot of their resources on things that don't bring value to them. They spend money on things that don't bring the money that they spend back to them.

The poor invest their time in liabilities. The poor spend their money on liabilities. The poor spend their money on things that others will think of them as rich. But they know that those things they spent on don't increase in value or bring returns. Liabilities are things that destroy your money. Liabilities don't bring returns. You cannot be financially free by spending your money on things that don't multiply your money.

Liabilities only take money from your pocket. They cost you a lot to maintain or keep them in the right status. Liabilities don't bring money. You continue to get into financial problems when you continue to put your money in liabilities. The poor spend their money on things that impress others and the rich spend their money on things that will make them more money. It is the spending pattern that separates the two.

- Your house

- Your car

- Your clothes

They don't necessarily prove you are rich or financially free. They only impress those without financial intelligence.

Your background affects what you spend money on. How you were brought up affects your spending habits. Take an audit of your spending habits over the last 10 years, if you are struggling now it means you have been spending your money on liabilities. Things that don't bring you money and things that do not increase in value over time. If you change that habit you will start to see progress in your finances.

.

CHAPTER 21

ᑕᐧ

ASSETS

One of the major evidences that show someone is financially intelligence is the assets that they have accumulated or invested in over many years. The rich have many income generating assets and they don't have to work to have money flow to them. When others are misusing their money the rich continue to focus on investing in assets that bring money with little effort or management.

What assets have you been investing in over the last 10 years or 20 years? It takes time to see the benefits from the assets that you invest in. Assets bring money to you and also increase in value over time. Once you have lots of assets that bring money to you more than you need you have become financially free. You make money by investing in assets. You save money to invest in assets. You build a business so that you can invest in other assets, the excess from the business.

You cannot be financially intelligent and have no assets to prove your intelligence. They have assets that cash flow more than what is spent on it. You can easily build different sources of income if you can build skills that can manage different assets you invest in.

- The wealthy invest in assets
- You become financially free by investing in assets
- Business is an asset
- Real estate is an asset
- Farmlands
- Cocoa farms etc.
- Assets work for you
- Assets must bring in more money than it is required to keep it
- You must have control over the assets
- Assets don't require a lot of effort to manage

You are an asset. Never forget to invest in yourself. Your financial intelligence. Your financial education. Your Network. The poor have no assets that bring in money. The average may just have some savings.

If you happen to not have a salary again can your assets take care of your financial needs without compromising your current living status?

If you want to become financially independent then focus on asset accumulation and keep at it for a long time. Keep doing that for the rest of your life. Accumulate assets tha generates income all the time.

CHAPTER 22

᠙

BUSINESSES

——————————

Creators, innovators and problems solvers in business are the ones who succeed financially. The others are those who are occupied with consumption. Financially intelligence and business go hand in hand. Those who build businesses are those who continually improve their financial intelligence. Financial intelligence is not so much about financial certificates and degrees. It has a lot to do with your ability to build financial freedom over time. There are steps, skills and discipline used to attain financial independence.

There is always something that is needed by other people and if you pay attention you can easily turn that need into business.

There is always something that is needed by other people and if you pay attention you can easily turn that need into business. Once you start that business you have to have the discipline and the modesty to grow it. You don't need to convince anybody that you are successful. Let the business grow and be ready to go beyond your comfort zone.

The path to financial freedom for the most part is on your ability to build a profitable business. That is the path we used. We had little opportunity to attain our financial freedom through employment or government positions so we started just like most people who build businesses.

We started small and with the little that we had. We had to be tough-minded and had to commit to personal development. Learned almost everything that was needed for us to be able to build the businesses that we built. It is not so much about the type of business, service or product, but it was about our commitment to the vision, owning businesses, investments and having financial freedom. This can be achieved by anybody who so desires to have financial freedom through entrepreneurship. It takes time. It takes a lot of effort but it works. It works beyond imagination. So look around you. What is it that is needed in your area that you can provide and charge for it? Start with it.

Be proud of it even if it is GH¢ 1 that you make for the first time. It is a seed and it will grows if you keep nurturing it.

Building business brings freedom, especially financial freedom that very few who don't build businesses experience. There is no entry barrier, no qualification is needed. Just your willingness and your relentlessness to stick to the vision. In our economy, everywhere is open for business. Open your eyes. Shine your eyes. If you are looking for opportunities in Ghana, look at business opportunities. Not employment opportunities. Refuse to convince yourself that you are not cut for business. What is basically done in business is problem solving and if you look around you there are problems that you can solve. That is the essence of your education.

It is to solve problems.

- Food problems
- Water problems
- Health problems
- Emotional problems
- Financial problems
- Technology problems
- Housing problems
- Fashion problems
- Identity problems
- Energy problems
- Many many problems

There are millions of problems that you can have a business out of. Just change the way you think about problems. When you see problems don't say someone else should come and solve them. You are the one to solve them. Provide solutions to problems that people can afford to pay you and you have a business. The other thing you can add as you subject yourself to getting knowledge as you build that business.

- Study about finance
- Study the entrepreneurship process
- Study how to build a team
- Study how a business system is built
- Study about selling
- Study about the culture of the people
- Study about technology
- Etc

It takes a lot of resilience to become successful in business. Be tough for the journey Start that business. Grow the business.

Stay with it and it will grow.

CHAPTER 23

INVESTMENTS

The wealthy invest while the rest of the people either only spend money or save money. Financial freedom comes from investing the money that comes to us in income-generating assets, vehicles that continually bring money. This is a major difference between those who make money work for them and those who work for money all the time.

They build businesses and they build different sources of income all the time. They are always investing their money. They are not the ones who waste money. They understand you have options when you have money. Real freedom cannot be devoid of financial freedom and those who have money understand this.

The best place to invest is in yourself. If you don't understand it you will soon lose it and so increase your financial intelligence. That is the way you protect your investment. Your financial knowledge, skill and discipline are the best security for your investment. You should have control over your investment and your investment should have positive cash flow. Your investment should grow in value and should be easy to manage. Have a long-term plan for your investments for at least 10 years and never forget to build great relationships as you build your investment. Your network is an investment as well. Wherever you spend your time, money and mind is where you are investing, so pay attention. Invest in ethics, truth and honesty. Don't steal or cheat to invest, it has no future. Patience is required as you invest. Your financial investment is your responsibility not the government. If you handle your investment you can choose not to work again in the future and so do it well. Study where to invest in our culture and our system. It is not that complex. Make it very simple.

- An entrepreneur's approach to investment is different from employees. An entrepreneur invests in businesses mainly.

- You can be an employee and still build investments which can lead to financial freedom

Learn to be innovative and creative in your investments and structure your investments. Real financial freedom comes from your investments, from real estate to agriculture to businesses to commodities. The options are many and the options are yours.

CHAPTER 24

FINANCIAL INDEPENDENCE

It takes making intelligent financial decisions to gain financial independence. There are financial laws that must be understood and put into practice for us to reach this goal. It takes a lot of effort to educate ourselves about finances to become financially free. Making intelligent

- Financial choices to amass wealth.
- Creating multiple streams of income.
- Knowing how to save money to invest.
- Multiplying the money.
- Knowing how to handle financial crises, debt management.
- Knowing what they call assets and liabilities.
- Understanding cash flow.

Being disciplined and credible with money are some of the things we must know to reach financial independence. We must have our own financial goals, must study our environment to know our financial culture, our financial systems, how our people behave with money and many more. Financial independence takes long term investment in assets that generate cash flow with very limited physical effort.

Live life knowing that your financial success is your responsibility. Don't renege this duty to anybody. Just like when you are sick you must be the one to take the medicine, know that you are the one to take this drug to be financial independence. Don't push it forward. Work on your finance as early as possible even if it has to start from your teens. It really does not matter your level of academic education, to have financial freedom you have place so much importance on financial literacy, discipline and freedom. It is not an easy path for many but it is achievable if you so desire to achieve this freedom. Don't forget that without financial free life is constantly difficult and controlled by those who have financial power over you. Those who pay you salary or give you financial support. Taking time to read this book means that you desire to improve your financial intelligence and your financial status. You can change your financial status as you have seen in this book by improving your

Work on your finance as early as possible even if it has to start from your teens.

financial education. Continue to improve your financial education and your financial skills and your financial intelligence will improve. You will see that life is entirely different for those who have such intelligence. Study our culture and what really works in terms of achieving your freedom. What many people don't study is the economic infrastructure that we have in our country. Focus on having control over your finances, different sources of income and the various investments that we can get involved in. Find something to sell. Start a business. Look at agriculture. If you look around you should see that the financial systems that made our grandparents and great-grandparents wealthy are still available to us. What we need is the wisdom they used to create those wealth. Apply modern technology and management on what we have and you will be financially free. Pursue financial independence. It is within your reach. Every one of us can reach somewhere in this journey if you are committed to it.

Focus on business and investment and you will be free. You will meet many challenges and problems but don't give up. Subject yourself to continuous learning and be resilient. Have higher sense of purpose, think long term, build great network of great achievers. Save money, have budget, see cash flow, multiply your resources, build businesses and invest for long term.

Your financial decisions and choices show the level of your financial intelligence and your financial independence.

CHAPTER 25

FUTURE

The future belongs to those who create it. What is it that you are building now that can that can bring you money when you can no more work or receive salary? What will take care of you? What will your children and grandchildren be financially. What will finances be when you can. The life that you see is the life you work for. Many employed people are told to retire around 65years but how do you retire when you have not income to take care of you. Are you are able to take care of yourself and those who depend on you when you have no source of income.

Remember, you don't need to be in your old age to have financial freedom. You can be financially free for the most part of your life if you are financially intelligent. Why people suffer financially is because of the level of their financial intelligence.

In fact your financial intelligence clearly shows when you are in your 60s or 70s. This time is when you energy is not as before and your finances may not be as strong as when you were working. Your health may start to have complications especially if you did not pay attention when you were young. It is a big problem when your finances and health start to have complications at the same time. Not enough money and not in good health. You must work against these two challenges as you age. Do you have any good financial vehicles that will help in your retirement age.

If you don't plan well you will face with this reality where you have to be calling others to help you with your hospital bills and drugs. If your children are fine financially they can help. The challenge is different when you don't have children or people who are fit financially to help you in your old age.

Don't take care of the future alone. The future of your partner as well, if you are married. The future of your family. Do it together. Plan it together and work it together. That future is not that far. The future starts today. You should not be shocked of what happens in that future. You can take care of that future today. The future is what you are doing today.

The future starts today.

Now that you have time and energy

- Invest in yourself
- Invest in your education

- Invest in businesses
- Invest in properties
- Invest in agriculture
- Invest in the your children
- Invest in your grand children
- Invest in others
- Invest in people
- Impact lives

Don't live your live as if that day will never come. If you don't die early you will be old and how you live when you are old shows how financially intelligent you have been all your life.

Pay attention to the next generation. Those who will take the baton from you. How are you educating them. Their general education. Their financial education. Can you help any of them to start business. If you can, do it. The seeds that you sow today will become big trees that you will benefit from when you need them most.

AFTERWORD

The financial knowledge you acquire, the skills you develop and the insight you gain out of you putting the knowledge into practice form your financial intelligence. It appears that most important things in life are not constructively taught. The things that we all will need to live are basically not taught in our institutions. They are not mainly part of our upbringing. So most of us would try to find those things out ourselves. Financial education is one of those most important things. When you look at decisions the people that we think have a lot of education make with money, it shows that a lot of us don't do anything about money. If you don't know much, you will not make any right decisions. We have been programmed. It is part of the script. Go to school. Look for a job. Get married. Buy a car. Build a house. Look for comfort. So majority of us will all our lives probably work and get salaries that we will never be enough. If you have the right information you can do much with the little that come to you. Ignorance is possibly the only thing that separates us from where we want to go. If anything can control you, if the economic system can control you, if anything controls humans, it's because they intentionally programmed them to be ignorant about that thing that they use to control the people. Your financial intelligence is the way out of this financial nightmare that many people deal with all their lives.

Many people hope that one day one day, they will get money. Most people hope that things will change and they will become rich. So that's like relying on lotto or hoping that a miracle will happen one day. Maybe they do. What I have seen, not many become rich by miracles. Once you improve your financial intelligence you will not have to worry about basic things in life. You don't have to worry about money when your child is sick. Not worry when the rent is due, you can at least pay for the rent. When the car breaks down, you can service it without worrying about your finances. As your financial intelligence improves you will know how to make money work for you and not you working for money all your life. You can live without waiting for monthly salary. Your financial intelligence is responsible for your financial freedom. Your business will do well as you improve in financial intelligence. How you spend money. Your savings. Your financial goals. How you think of liabilities. How you invest in Assets. How you even invest for your future and the future of those who come out of you. Your financial intelligence affect how many lives you are able to impact. Your fulfilment in life.

Made in the USA
Monee, IL
20 October 2024

68372527R00056